This Creatures of the World Series Book belongs to:

____

In Antarctica, You'll Find Me

is a great book series to begin your journey of learning about the different types of animals in the world.

Thank you for your support.

ISBN-13: **978-1727421064**

This book is dedicated,

To our first born Adam, Dream big but love bigger. Love always mom and dad.

To Raelyn Rose M. and Michael Allen M. you are precious in every way, the sunshine
of our day. You both are the joy in our soul and the loves of our lives,
love your mama and dada.

To my children Chris, Mia, Sophia, Dora, Omar. Always be yourself, encourage one
another, and build each other up. We are so proud to be your parents. We love you
all, Mom and Dad

To Arissel you are the most wonderful, courageous, beautiful blessing we could
have ever hoped for. We love you, Mom and Dad.

To our beautiful, smart, and kind Chloe, never stop dreaming or give up hope.
Always shine and be positive to achieve your goals in life.
We love you, mommy and daddy.

This book is dedicated,

To Olivia,
        Nezy,
            Lucas,
                and Sapphire 
                        we love you to the moon and back!

                                        -Grandpa & Grandma

In Antarctica You'll Find Me

Written and Illustrated by:
Lillie Gamez

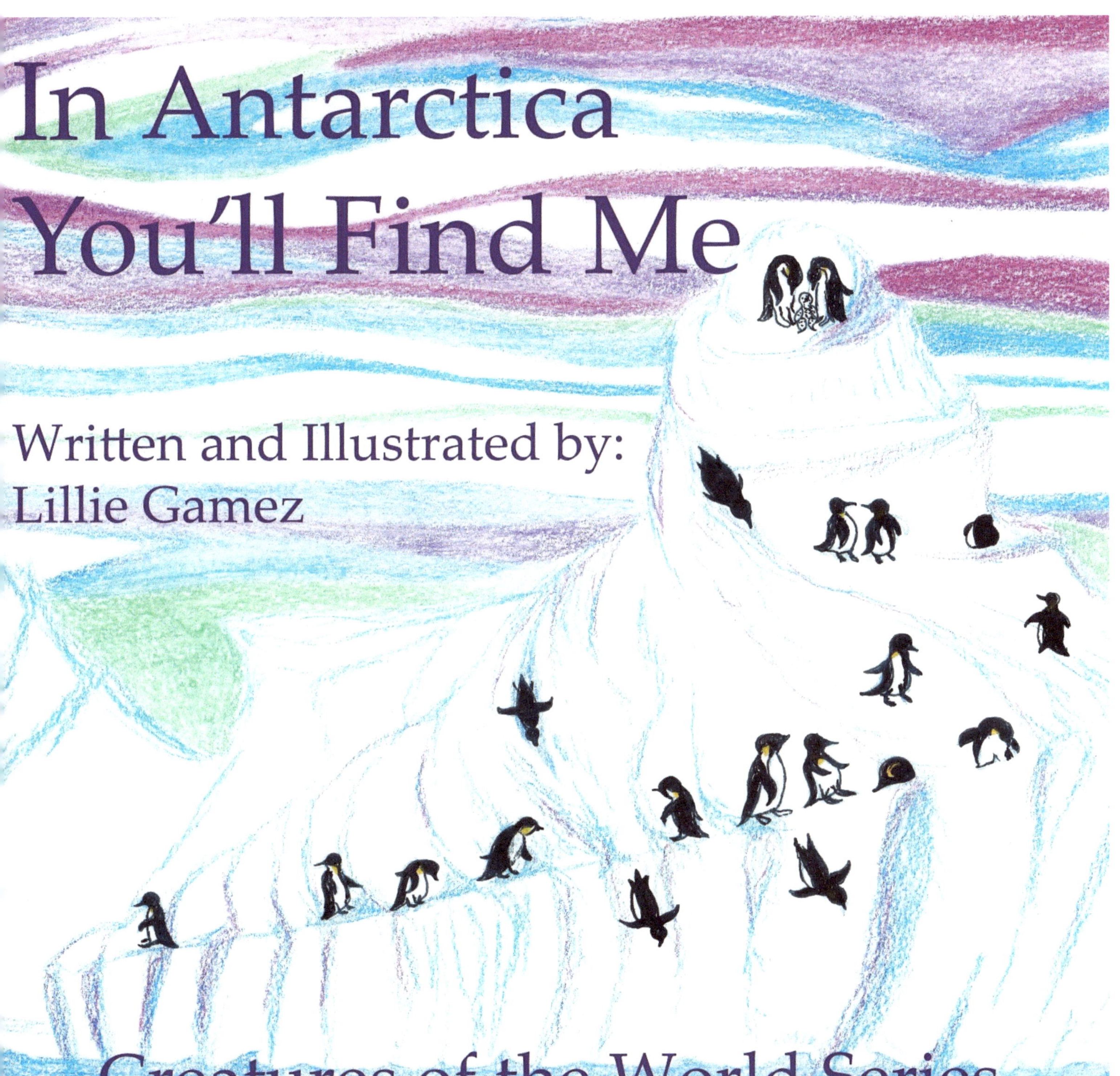

Creatures of the World Series

In Antarctica, you'll find me. Flying high with the largest wings you ever did see. I am a wandering Albatross on a long fishing trip I will be.

In Antarctica, you'll find me on land or in the sea. As a snow seal, I use my whiskers to find my food. Eating fish and squid are my favorite things to do.

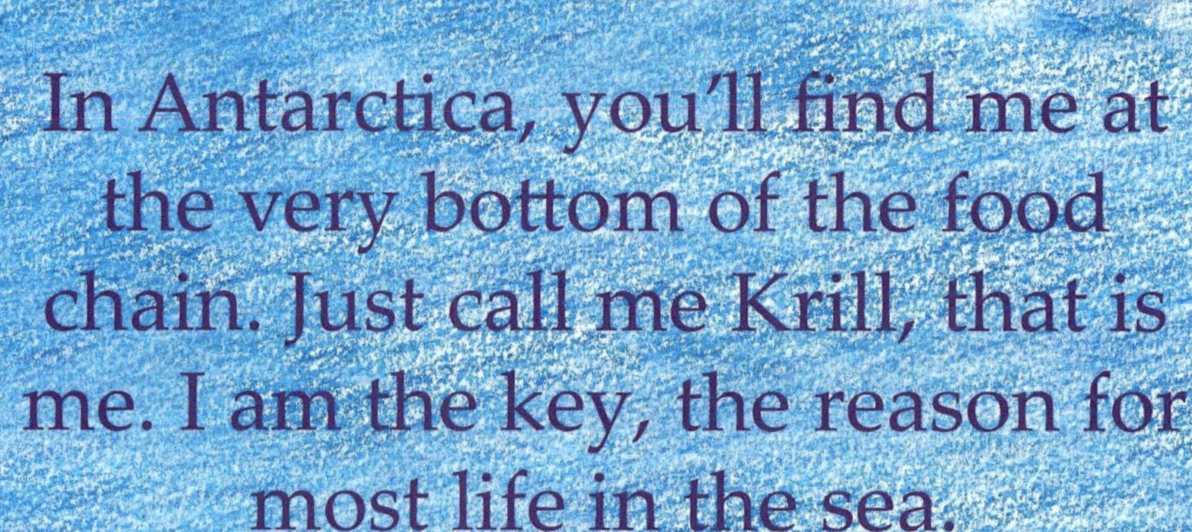

In Antarctica, you'll find me at the very bottom of the food chain. Just call me Krill, that is me. I am the key, the reason for most life in the sea.

In Antarctica, you'll find me.
A Polar bear sitting pretty
with my tiny ears. Keeping
warm with my fuzzy fur and
my pups around me.

In Antarctica, you'll find me. An Emperor Penguin with scale-like feathers that protect me. As a papa, I keep my egg warm as my lady love brings food to our baby and I.

In Antarctica, you'll find me.
Squawking saying, "Hey! Look
at me!" I am the South Pole
Skua, always near my nest to
keep my eggs safe with my
mate not far from me.

In Antarctica, you'll find me.
Two ivory tusks and a
mustache on me. I am a
walrus, don't you see. I can
live up to forty years if a polar
bear doesn't eat me.

In Antarctica, you'll find me.
Traveling along with my
small orca whale community.
As a family, we love to feast,
eating seals and other kinds of
whales outside the family.

Long ago in Antarctica, you would have found me wandering. Eating all the plants that my eyes could see. Trinisaura was my name and being small and fast was my game.

Draw your favorite Antarctic

Creature in the space above.

The Author and Illustrator of this wonderful Creatures of the World Series, is Lillie Leonor Gamez. A retired Art Teacher hoping to inspire families everywhere to love animals and create their own works to share with the world. Born and raised in Del Rio, Texas, Gamez received a Bachelor's degree of Fine Arts in Photography from Texas State University. She is currently homeschooling her two young children and using everyday life as inspiration to create her next series. You can also find her teaching art at different local community centers. For more information about her services, check out her website at

www.OnlineMamaG.com

and sign up for the next event near you.